"The book contains a lot of i
would apply no matter wha
There is a lot of common sens
of especially in the area of ps)
with people."

Bobby Shew, jazz trumpeter, 30 albums,
played with Buddy Rich, Woody Herman,
Maynard Ferguson

"John and Angela Taylor's new book *Band Aide* is an
excellent book for those struggling with the in's and out's
of both starting and running a band. Told from first hand
experience, their advice is well thought out and clear.
While revealing the pitfalls of the band business, they also
propose excellent solutions to the challenges facing new
band leaders. They seem to have thought of everything.
Bravo!"

Roy Poper, trumpeter on recording sessions
with B.B. King, Frank Zappa, and The
Mothers of Invention, has more than 2000
motion picture soundtracks for major
Los Angeles studios. He is recorded on
the Crystal, Orion, Nonesuch and Dorian
labels and is a faculty member of Oberlin
College Conservatory of Music.

"It's about time for a book to come out that can help young musicians, new bands, and established bands know how to get it together so they can work, perform, and stay together — so when it's time to record, they can go in the studio and know what to do, not wasting time and money — and eliminate the frustrations of being uninformed and unprepared. This book, I believe, will provide invaluable insight into good musicianship and dealing successfully in the entertainment business. Having been a musician for the last 40 years, owning and managing Pulpit Recording Studios in Lancaster, CA and gigging with some of the greatest such as Billy Higgins, Archie Shepp, Mike B. Le Flea of The Hot Chili Peppers, Norman Conners, Oliver Lake, Beaver Harris, Dewey Redmon, Juliajn Priester, Bishop Norman Williams, Mel Martin, George Coleman, Eddie Marshal, James Leary, Water Davis, Jr., Smiley Winters, San Francisco All-Star Bands, Tequila Mockingbird — and many more, I know that this book will be an invaluable tool for up-and-coming creative musicians everywhere."

Pastor Eddie Edwards,
formerly known as Snakepit Eddie

BAND AIDE

A BAND AND GIG
SURVIVAL GUIDE
(INSIGHTS FROM INSIDERS)

John and Angela Taylor

BOOKS FOR ALL THAT YOU ARE

PERSONHOOD PRESS

Published by
Personhood Press
"Books for All that You ARE!"
PO Box 370
Fawnskin, CA 92333
800-429-1192
personhoodpress@att.net
www.personhoodpress.com

Band Aide
A Band and Gig Survival Guide (Insights from Insiders)
By John and Angela Taylor

ISBN: 1-932181-17-2

Cover Design: Linda Jean Thille

Graphic Art: C.D. Bailey and Linda Jean Thille

Design and Layout: Linda Jean Thille

Editor: Susan Remkus

Printed in the United States of America

First Printing, May 2005

ACKNOWLEDGMENTS

It would be much too long of a list to name all
of those who helped us out emotionally and financially
developing and writing this book.
You all know who you are!
From the deepest, deepest region
from the bottom of our hearts...
Thank you so very, very much!
We love you all!

Angie and John Taylor

PREFACE

Hello fellow musicians and singers!!! We wrote this book to possibly spare you some of the headaches, heartaches, and challenges that we have encountered in hiring musicians, running rehearsals, and dealing with situations at gigs. This book is for every age group because these situations can crop up no matter how old or young you are. Our intention was to present these situations in a casual and easy to read style. The question/answer format gets right to the point and allows you to readily find the topic and information that you might be looking for.

You can read this book in any order you want to. And yes, every situation has really happened to us! These are real-life experiences!!!

Our email address is in the back of this book if you would like to contact us. You will also find an order form for our original, easy listening CD.

*We wish you the best on your musical
journey throughout life!*

John and Angela Taylor

TABLE OF CONTENTS

SECTION 1

Keys to finding musicians with whom you're compatible

Topics

SECTION 2

Rehearsal and band rules

Topics

Song rules and band name

Topics

SECTION 3

Where the gigs are and how to get them

Topics

SECTION 4

Before the gig

Topics

Situations at the gig

Topics

Money Issues and Getting Paid

Topics

After the gig

Topics

SECTION 5

How to make a CD from your house 90

SECTION 6

How to get your songs picked up by a music publisher, cable TV, video CD-ROM companies, and radio stations 94

SECTION 7

Tips on being a leader

Topics

SECTION 8

Writing Charts for the Band:
"To chart or not to chart,
that is the question."

SECTION 1

Keys to finding musicians
with whom
you're compatible

Hiring musicians who are older/younger
or your own age

We have found that hiring in our own age range works out the best for us. This is because we all grew up with the same music, have a love for it, and are highly familiar with how each song should be played or sung. Plus, we can discuss matters relevant to our age group. We know bands that have a very diverse age range and everyone seems happy, but it seems that most often, musicians form bands within their own age group. Whatever you do, make sure the musicians can play the music and have a love for it—and that they're not just in your band for some quick money to tide them over until they find a band they really want to be in.

Older players more "emotionally
mature" than younger ones?

It would seem that older musicians have learned how to handle their emotions pretty well, since most of them have been through many band/stage circumstances that have taught them how to act appropriately, but this is not always the case. We've had older musicians who resorted to childish revenge, ego trips, temper tantrums and the like. You can't always assume that older musicians have a more stable emotional base than younger ones.

Are older musicians "better players"
than younger ones?

If you can play, you can play. It doesn't matter if you are 16 or 60. Someone may have played their guitar for 30 years and not be as good as someone who has only played for five years. Don't look at age as any barometer. You must hear the person and decide for yourself. This goes for listening to singers, too. Age and experience are no guarantee of performance quality.

"Professionally educated musicians" versus "street musicians"

It doesn't make any difference who you hire as long as they can play what you need. We've had musicians with doctorates in Music who were no better than someone who had learned to play his instrument on his own. It is the result that counts. Recruit someone who delivers what you want, irrespective of formal qualifications.

Hiring rich versus poor musicians

Don't be led astray by anyone's equipment or gig connections. We've always chosen musicianship over someone's social or economic status. No amount of money can make up for bad musicianship. There is no guarantee that the prestige of the performer is related to musicianship. Judge only by results.

Hiring a mix of professionals and amateurs in the same band

Unless the inexperienced musicians are quick learners, it is inadvisable to mix the experienced with the less experienced, unless you are all patient dudes and don't mind this. The inexperienced musicians may never get up to the level of the rest of the band. All you can do is try them out and see how fast they can progress.

Hiring someone who is "only in it for the money"

It is emotionally rewarding when everyone's heart is into the music, plus the audience feels this, as well. You may find a great musician who can play your tunes but you know his heart is not into the music and that he is really only in the band for some gig money. It has been our experience that musicians who don't care about the music will leave and find another band to be in. Sure, there are probably some musicians who just love to gig and don't care what type of music they are playing, as long as they are on stage. These musicians could possibly last a long time in a band.

Hiring someone who likes your style of music but keeps suggesting other styles to play

Let's say you play only 50s music and you hire someone who says they love all eras of music. This is fine. We all like many eras of music. But if you want a strictly 50s band you need to enforce this immediately or you will risk the musician trying to get you to do music from the 60s/70s/80s once he feels comfortable that he has been accepted into the band. He might even be adamant about it. So enforce your era of music from the get-go. We have had this happen many times, that's why we bring it up.

Hiring musicians who live locally or far away

Avoid, if you can, hiring musicians from afar because they eventually will quit in favor of their local bands. Imagine the difficulty and expense of going to distant rehearsals (especially if low on gas money!). Dedicated, loyal, but long-distance musicians are the exception rather than the rule on this matter.

Hiring musicians who were "famous" years ago

These people do not guarantee success. On one hand, the mention of their names may attract an audience. Moreover, their knowledge, experience, and professional connections can be a boon, provided they respect you as a manager. On the other hand, they may become domineering and unmanageable. Their arrogance may result in their absences at rehearsals, for they think they are "beyond that." You need to audition them like everyone else. Don't assume they can still sing or play their instrument up to the level they used to.

Hiring back-up musicians in case the others don't work out

Yes, it is a good idea to have back-ups because your regular musicians can get sick, have to work overtime at jobs, have family crises, or just quit. Always keep a list of musicians' phone numbers that you have auditioned previously.

Rehiring someone you previously fired

We have re-hired two people we'd previously fired. One person really tried hard to do what was required and he worked out well. The other musician just couldn't quite cut it and had to be re-fired.

We all know that no one is perfect. You are going to have to put up with flaws from everyone, just like they have to put up with your flaws. But the flaws cannot be too far-out from what you require.

Some musicians are not that great in playing their instrument but can sing or speak to the audience well. Other musicians may be somewhat arrogant but are great players. You simply have to hire (or re-hire) people who are as close to what you are looking for as possible, and hope they can stay and grow with the band.

Hiring people who used to have their own band together

We've tried this a few times. It was fun, at first, to have a few band members from another band join our band. All of them knew each other and had a good friendship. The only thing you have to watch for is this group trying to make your band, "their" band. That is, they group together and try to get you to change the band to what their band used to be like. If they can all respect you and follow your vision for your band, that is good. The difficult part comes when you have to fire one of them for some reason and his friends get mad at you. You can let them all go at once if you feel you need a total re-haul/clean start. It's all up to you. We are just pointing out what can happen.

Hiring friends and family members

You should know these people well and know what to expect from them musically and emotionally. Make sure they can follow the vision you have set for the band and let them know that breaking the rules is not allowed just because they are friends or family. For example, they shouldn't show up late or not learn their parts because they think you might overlook these faults.

The best ways we have found musicians fast

- Calling up friends/family to ask if they know a guitarist etc.

- Asking around at your job, church, school, college etc.

- Hanging a sign in music stores—Bass Player Wanted etc.

- Putting an ad on the internet at www.musicians.com

- Putting an ad in a free, local newspaper

- Posting an ad at colleges (if you want younger musicians)

Posting an ad in music stores has been where we get most of our responses.

Note: Someone who plays well at rehearsal may freeze on stage. A musician or singer may be fantastic at rehearsals, but put him on stage and he may freeze and do a terrible job, due to stage fright. This is where hiring someone who says they have lots of experience on stage can help. Now, even though they may say they are totally experienced on stage, you won't really know until you are at the gig. Sometimes, people who have never been on stage will have no stage fright at all. So don't discount those people. Again, the gig reveals it all.

What to put in your
"Looking for Musician" ad/flyer

WANTED:

BASS PLAYER FOR 60's BAND
(Urgent – for upcoming Gigs*)
(*put if this is true)

– BAND PICTURE –

Call John – phone number

When musicians call you, *then* give more details. On the phone, we try to hit on the major things we need most. Once someone comes over for rehearsals, we get into more of the specifics.

What we tell musicians when they call

- Who is in the band now, what instruments they play, and if they sing.

- Rehearsals: when/where/length of time, and breaks.

- Whose PA system to bring to the gigs/ rehearsals.

- What types of gigs we do (classy or dives or both).

- What pay range our gigs are usually in (you must get this clear, because a musician can complain later that you are not booking the band for enough money). You must tell them if you do free gigs. Some musicians will not do these.

- Where our gigs are normally located: local or far away. (Make sure they can travel if you have faraway gigs.)

- We tell them we do outdoor gigs in the hot sun and cold weather and ask if they have any objection to playing those.

- We mention that we perform as a duo/trio if the rest of the band isn't available for a certain gig and ask if they would have a problem with that.

- We tell them the songs/artists we cover, plus original tunes we may perform. We let them know that if their originals fit the style of music, they can perform them at the gig, as well.

- We ask if they sing or play more than one instrument.

- We ask if family or jobs will hold them back.

- We tell them we perform like the artists on the CD but that sometimes we do improvise on certain songs.

- We tell them we don't always follow the set list and call songs out at gigs for the musicians to play.

- We mention that some gigs have a dress code and we can't always dress in jeans for gigs.

- We set up an audition for them.

Note: Just do the best you can in hiring musicians. Sometimes, people you never think would work out well actually do work out great, and people you thought would be with you forever are gone. Have a back-up list of people who previously showed interest in your band, so you are not caught off-guard if someone in your band gets sick, quits etc

SECTION 2

Rehearsal and band rules
Song rules and band name

Be clear who the leader is, from the get-go

If you are the leader, you must explain to your band that you have the final say on certain issues. For example, you may want the final say on: choice of songs, how the song is sung or played, who you hire and fire, at what types of gigs you want the band to perform, and more. This doesn't mean you don't listen to the input of the musicians, but someone has to have the final say or the band will never get off the ground, plus there will be constant arguing as to who does what.

We had a musician who helped us re-form our old band and thought he was a co-leader and could never be fired. Although this person was helpful to the band, he seemed to disappear when any of the tough issues came up, such as firing band members, dealing with problems at gigs or rehearsals, etc. He was never a co-leader in our minds, and we never asked him to help us on the tough issues. When it came time to let him go (because he didn't learn his parts), he wouldn't leave the band. He thought it was his band and he had equal say. After much heated debate, he finally left. Don't let this happen to you. Be clear who the leader is and what the duties are.

You start the band and the other musicians take over

You may be the one who started the band, only to find out that the other band members take over and start calling the shots. You must always assert yourself and make decisions, or others will walk all over you. Know your vision for the band in regard to the style of music, what types of gigs you play, who sings what, etc., and enforce these decisions early on. If you wait to enforce your rules, it will be too late and the other band members will have taken over and fired you.

Rehearsals: date, time, place, length, and breaks

You have probably already informed your musicians on these issues when they called to come over, but you may have forgotten to mention you have break-time at rehearsal. Some people need to smoke or whatever and it's good to allow a break time.

Start the rehearsals on time, or allow some slack time?

We usually cut people a ten-minute slack time on showing up for rehearsals, but no more than that. It's great if everyone can show up exactly on time, but we have found this just isn't reality. Anyone who is consistently late more than 15 minutes will be spoken to. It's not fair to the other band members to see a latecomer strolling in, setting up his equipment while everyone else is already set up and ready to practice.

Loudness level at rehearsals

Even if the neighbors allow loud playing, it may be too loud for some band members to tolerate. You should all agree on a loudness level; the leader should bring up the subject and you can all discuss.

Ending rehearsals on time

You need to end the rehearsal when you say you are going to. If you feel everyone wants to stay longer, ask. Make sure you don't assume they want to play longer just because you do. A lot of musicians have jobs and family; if you keep rehearsing without letting them leave on time, you may not find them staying in your band.

Don't let musicians leave
their equipment at your house

Even if you have renter's/home insurance, which covers damage and theft, you don't want another's equipment left at your house because if you fire that person, they may take a long time to pick up their equipment. We had someone who left their instruments at our house for two months, hoping we would hire him back. He didn't have any upcoming gigs so he didn't need his instruments. It wasn't until we told him we would have to put his instruments in the garage because they were in the way that he finally came for them. Another reason you don't want equipment left is that if you fire someone, you have to see him again when he comes to pick up his instruments, and that can be awkward.

When a band member wants you
to pay them to rehearse

Yes, this really happens, and some band members feel that their time is too valuable to come up to your house and rehearse for free.

Also, there are situations in which a band member is really broke and doesn't have the gasoline to come over, and wants you to pay for it.

It's up to you what you want to do.

Allowing your band members to play
in other bands

We allow band members to play in other bands, but if they cancel our gigs to take another band's gigs, this is not right. We understand if a band member gets some huge Vegas gig with another band and wants to do that for a weekend; that's fine. He just needs to let us know so we can get a sub. We are not going to stop anyone from making good money somewhere else. But if the band member is consistently putting our band on the back burner, he is considered a "substitute" in our band and we would find someone more permanent.

What to do if someone is consistently late for rehearsals

Being late is not fair to the other band members. When the band is already playing a song and the late person is setting up his equipment, the leader needs to ask why he is late. Further, the leader should find out if the rehearsals would be more convenient at another time or a different day of the week.

Another way to handle latecomers is to say nothing to them but tell the other band members to show up at the same time the late person does. Thus, you are all on time.

Don't let band members cancel rehearsal at the last minute!

If your band members can't make rehearsal, have them call the band in plenty of time. Maybe the rehearsal can be rescheduled for another day or time. For example, let's say the bass player was going to cancel. The bass player may think, "Well, they don't really need me there because the keyboard player can play left-hand keyboard bass." But maybe the drummer really needed the real bass player there to work up a better rhythm section; the left-hand piano bass isn't going to be a replacement for this. No one should cancel at the last minute unless it's an emergency.

When a band member keeps missing rehearsals

Musicians miss rehearsals for these three reasons:

- They really can't make it, due to jobs or family

- They feel they don't need to rehearse, they know it all

- They don't feel like coming over that day or night

It's good to have everyone at rehearsal. Even if a musician does know all the songs, the other band members may need this person there to help them practice. It also helps the band members get to know one another and have a friendly stage presence, instead of looking like a "pick-up band" where no one knows each other (they all show up at a gig and hope for the best). The audience can sense if the band members look like they belong together or are just on stage for the money.

Once, we allowed an exceptionally great guitarist to only show for the gigs, with no rehearsals. Although the other band members would have loved for this person to rehearse with us, he just would not do it. The band all agreed to go along with this situation and see if it was worth it. For a while, it was. But then we found someone who was more local, friendlier with all of us, and although not exceptional in guitar (as was our genius), did a great job anyway. We hired him on.

Too much joking/chit-chat and not enough band practice

Jokes and chit-chat are great and help people laugh and break the ice. But you may find that nothing gets done. Also, some band members may like the jokes/chat and others may resent it. It's up to the leader to control the situation and keep people on track. We usually tell people to chat and joke while they are setting up their equipment and while they are tearing it all down. Sure, some chat or jokes during rehearsal is totally okay, but not all the time. The leader must nicely interrupt and get the band back to the songs they were working on. For example, the leader can say, "Hey, that was really funny, thanks for sharing that. But let's get back to working on the blues tune."

Too much seriousness/perfectionism, not enough fun!!!

Wow, this can be a drag, as well. When things aren't fun, most musicians will find other bands to be in. Sure, you may be getting a lot of work accomplished and tunes performed correctly, but if the atmosphere is too serious —no one smiling or chatting at all—the band will feel like a burden. The audience can tell if band members are unhappy or stressed, so lighten up and allow some chit-chat and jokes (preferably before or after rehearsal, but allow some during band practice).

When someone does not learn their parts for the next rehearsal

Sometimes things come up and a band member simply cannot get his parts down for the next rehearsal. You do not want this to become a regular habit, however. If everyone knows their parts but this one person, it holds up the band's progress. The leader will have to probe into why the problem is occurring and see if the band member can correct the situation.

Musician forgets to bring lyrics/charts/glasses etc. to rehearsal

We always have extras of these things. If a band member says they cannot sing a song because they forgot their lyrics, we pull out a copy of the lyrics. A band member once showed up without his glasses and lyrics. Having a computer right there at rehearsal, we printed the lyrics in huge 28 point font so he could read them. He had volunteered to sing this tune a week ago; why was he so unprepared? I wondered if the "I forgot the lyrics and glasses" was an excuse to get out of doing the song. We let the issue slide and he never came unprepared again. Now, if you don't have extra lyrics, charts, or whatever a band member keeps forgetting, it's confrontation time!

When band members don't get along at rehearsals

Nothing is worse than having two band members you really like and want in the band who don't get along at all. Sometimes fights happen so fast it's hard to know who did what or said what and know who to blame for it. For us, after many rehearsal fights and two fights on stage between two of our band members, it became clear who was the main instigator and we let him go (see the "If there is a fight on stage between band members" section for what to do on gig fights). How do you help the two fighters get along at rehearsal? Well, the leader has to step in and stop the fight, saying something like, "Hey, let's all calm down and discuss who is singing/playing the wrong notes" or "Let's take a short break and come back to this issue when we are all in a calmer state." The leader then needs to try to find out what's going on between the two band members.

Try not to have these two musicians stand near each other at rehearsal or on stage. Oftentimes, this alone can really help solve your problem.

Rehearse-a-holic band members who never learn their parts, yet want to rehearse all the time

We had one band member who always wanted to have rehearsals, since he knew he needed improvement. We agreed to this but then found out that having constant rehearsals didn't make him improve any faster than having less rehearsal time. Anyone who holds up the band's progress on a continuous basis won't last. Some musicians want constant rehearsals because that's the only way they learn their parts. They don't want to learn them on their own. If you can get everyone together to rehearse a lot, fine, but most people have jobs/families/school and don't have time for so many rehearsals.

Band members who buy expensive equipment to make up for lack of talent

Funny thing we've noticed is that sometimes, but not all the time, band members who have lots of expensive equipment really are making up for lack of talent. They keep buying new piece after new piece in the hope it will improve their performance. Just because another band member has lots of expensive equipment does not mean that he made tons of money from playing gigs. Don't be fooled by "Expensive equipment = Talent."

Band members who go out and buy new equipment to secure their place in a new band

Another funny thing we've noticed is that we've had band members—usually the less talented—go out and buy expensive equipment right when they got hired into the band. They tell all the band members how much their items cost and that they bought everything especially for the band. Although it's nice that they care about the band and want to have equipment that sounds good, it is also a way for them to try to secure their permanent place. How can you fire someone who just went out and bought boatloads of new stuff for the band? Well, you can still fire them if they can't play the material, so don't let anyone guilt-trip you by trying to buy their way into the band.

Fill-in band members (subs) who put your band down

At rehearsal, we found out our bass player couldn't make the next few gigs. We hired a fill-in bass player (sub) for these gigs. The sub had his own band but agreed to participate in a few gigs of ours. He was an excellent musician but no better than the rest of us. Yet he consistently put down everyone in the band in a sarcastic way. We are open to constructive criticism, but this was evil. Here we were, giving him gigs he needed (his band was not booked on those weekends) and all he could do was complain about us! Turns out, he was jealous of all of us and thought our band would snuff his band out eventually. His band and our band do perform the same style of music and gig at the same types of places. Apparently, he wanted to take the money from our gigs and put us down as much as he could, to try to dissuade us from booking more gigs. It's hard to believe people like that exist, but they do!

Band meeting (before or after rehearsal) or another day?

We think it's best to have a band meeting after everyone has rehearsed, because music puts everyone in a good mood. You don't have to officially sit down and interrogate anyone. You can all talk in the rehearsal room in a friendly way and have drinks and pizza. Sure, you can have a day set aside for a band meeting if you can get everyone to come over for it.

Band meeting through email?

Well, we think discussing lightweight issues can work, as long as everyone types clearly so as not to be misunderstood. With heavy issues that can bring up anger and misunderstandings, emails can bring confusion. There is nothing worse than misinterpreting an email and typing an angry retort when the other person wasn't saying anything bad to begin with! For example: In something as simple as "Please remember to bring your charts," musicians can read this as if you were treating them like little children. They may see sarcasm, when all you were doing was making a friendly reminder. You can preface statements by putting it this way, "I am saying this in a friendly tone for you all to please remember to bring your charts." This leaves no room for misinterpretation about your tone of voice.

How to tell someone their faults one-on-one

You can tell someone their faults without hurting their feelings. Compliment them first and tell them how much you appreciate them being in the band. Then tell them you'd like some improvement in whatever area. You can do this via email or phone, or before band practice—whichever route you want to take. Make sure that after you share your criticism with the person that you again tell them the positive things they have done in the band. Always end the discussion on a positive note. If you leave someone totally discouraged, chances are they will quit.

How to tell someone their faults in front of the band

At band practice the leader has to let the musicians know who is playing the song wrong, and correct the problem. If the leader doesn't catch this, another band member will bring it up. The leader needs to correct the problem in a helpful, nice, non-condemning way. Now, if the band member just can't get it played/sung correctly after many tries, the leader can tell him to practice the part for next rehearsal and go on to the next tune. If the gig is the next day and you have to get the part played correctly right away, keep going over the tune to get it right, if you have time. You may have to make the band rehearsal longer or have that one person stay longer and work on the part with you alone. If they can't seem to get the part down correctly and it doesn't look like they ever will, drop the tune from your set list, or tell the person to play his part a little softer than the rest of the band and not to play on the parts he doesn't know. If you are playing a gig where this would really be noticed, maybe you won't want to include that song. But if it is a big dance/food gig, he can get away with playing his part softer than the rest of the band.

Don't speak for another band member's opinion

Sometimes if you speak for a band member who is not present and say, "Well, Joe really likes this or hates that about a certain song," the band members will think that this is really your opinion on the matter. Best to have Joe speak for himself on whatever issues are bothering him or issues he likes.

Then again, sometimes you do have to speak up for what you think a musician would or should do, if that person is not present at rehearsal. Let's say Joe, the bass player, couldn't attend the rehearsal and you are going over a tune for which you think Joe would like to do a bass solo. The other band members don't agree with you that Joe would want to do this. For the sake of moving the rehearsal along, include the bass solo if you feel strongly that Joe would want it. Be sure to tell the band members that Joe will speak for himself on this matter at the next rehearsal.

How to fire a band member (phone, email, or in person)

If you can, try to remain somewhat friendly to the person you fire. You may fire someone thinking you can replace him with someone better, only to find this "better musician" doesn't exist, or if he does exist he wants more pay than the rest of the band. You may also run into the fired musician at a job interview, or see his new band playing at the stage next to you at a fair. You may then find out that he is what you want to have in your band and re-hire him once again.

The fired band member should have been warned a few times about what he was doing wrong. As for firing someone via phone, email, or in person, that is up to you. We have usually fired people by phone or email because we don't run into band members during the work week to fire them in person.

Should you fire a band member if you have already given him gigs?

If you have already given your band the upcoming gig schedule and feel you have to fire a band member or two, this is fine if they're not living up to what was expected of them. What we are saying is that, yes, you can take the gigs away from them. But you need to explain why these gigs are being taken away. Give them a chance to explain themselves first. When we took gigs away from a guitar player who never showed up for rehearsals, he found out who his replacement was and called that person and said he stolen his gigs and wanted them back. He thought that if he could get the new person to quit, he would be hired back. Gosh, people will resort to anything.

Should you fire a musician because you came across a better player?

Let's say you have a pretty decent guitar player, but by happenstance, you come across a fantastic guitar player who really wants to be in your band. You analyze your present guitar player and find he has followed all the rules of the band and there really isn't any reason to let him go—except that you found someone who plays better. Now, you don't actually know if this new person will follow band rules, so hiring him is taking a risk. Plus, if your present guitar player is a relatively decent player and individual, too, it's going to be hard to tell him you are suddenly letting him go.

If you really feel this new guitar player will take your band to the top and that you must have him no matter what the risk, that decision is up to you. You will have to explain this to your present guitar player. What you could do is tell your guitar player you really want to try this new person out on the next gig or two and that you feel you just must do this. My band usually does not take risks like this; if we are happy with the guitar player we have, we keep him. There is something to be said about having someone who is a friend, responsible, plays well, and follows the rules. But it truly is up to you. Many bands will replace their band members for better players. Sometimes it takes them to the top and sometimes it doesn't.

Tips on firing

If you have gigs that pop up and need to be filled right away, then of course, tell your band members so you can all rehearse. But don't tell them about any gigs you may have booked far off in the future. Your band members can change a few months down the road. Keep the far-off gigs quiet if you can, or only tell trusted band members—who you are sure will last that long in your band—about these gigs.

Song rules and band name

Who decides on what songs to choose for the band

Generally speaking, it should be a group decision; everyone agrees on what cover tunes or originals you all want to perform. Try not to play songs that a band member truly hates. There are so many songs out there to choose from within your style of music, you should be able to find suitable songs you all like.

Once in a while, I will sing a song I hate, only because the band members and audience just love the song, but I try not to make a rule of doing this. It's best you all love the tunes you do.

Don't take someone's word that they can sing well

I've had people tell me they sang with famous people or had their own hits out in the past, so I assumed they could still sing. But this is not always the case. You must hear someone sing in person and not from some CD they put out years ago—or even a week ago. If you assign songs to someone you have not yet heard sing, it's going to feel awkward telling them—once you do hear them sing—that it's not going to work out. If you can't take the songs away from this person, put their songs in the last set at the gig. This way, the band has already been accepted by the audience, and no one may care much what happens in the last set.

Should you perform a band member's original tunes?

If the original tune fits the style of music you are doing, it could work out well. We have performed some of our original tunes and our band members' original tunes with much success. We put some tunes in the last set if we weren't sure they would go over well in the first few sets. Since the band was accepted in the first three sets, the audience was not going to care if an original tune bombed in the last set.

No matter where on the set list you put the original tune, sandwich it between two great songs that everyone loves. The audience will hear a song they love and if the original tune bombs out next, you pick up the pace again with another great tune. If you are sure the original tune is going to be a smash, put it higher up on the set list and don't sandwich it in between two great songs.

Playing the song like the record/CD, or improvising a lot?

The leader of the band should make it known if he wants the songs played like the CD/record. Sometimes a band member won't play it like the record but it sounds great anyway; everyone in the band is happy, and so is the audience. Then again, if the musician is doing his own thing and improvising to the point that the song isn't recognizable, the leader must step in and tell the musician to play it like the record—or at least as close to the record as possible.

Deciding who sings lead or harmony

We go around the room and see how each person sounds singing the song or harmony. You'd be surprised that sometimes the weakest singer in the band can really pull certain songs off better than the great singers in the band. Give everyone a shot at singing. Don't let the better singers hog all the songs.

If you have to make a decision on the spot as to who will sing what song, say, "These are the parts I am assigning now and we shall see how they work out." If you are not sure who should sing what, and you don't have to decide right then and there, wait. Tell everyone you will let them know, via phone or email, what you have decided. Let them know that these parts can be changed in the future. It's also a good idea to have two band members learn the same songs if they can sing it equally well, in case one doesn't show for a gig. Or have one of them sing that song at the next gig, and the other sing it at the gig that follows.

Note: When harmony parts are finally locked in at a rehearsal, make sure they are memorized and/or documented on paper so that the next gig or rehearsal isn't spent starting from scratch re-learning the parts. Some musicians are better at harmony parts than others. Nonetheless, it can be extremely time-consuming (and no fun!) to keep going over harmony parts that were already worked out before.

What if someone who really can't sing, insists on singing?

You know, we have had someone who can't sing and really wanted to sing, so we let him sing a song or two in the last set at a casual dance gig. At dance gigs, no one is watching the band under a microscope—they're all dancing or eating. It's good to give the band member a very popular dance song everyone knows and loves. If the audience hears a song they love, sometimes they don't even care who is singing it, as long as the musicians play the song well. The song must be a fast dance tune for him to sing, because with the loud dance beat, no one is really paying that much attention to the vocals (like they would in a slow ballad, which showcases a person's voice more and puts the band in the background). At least the band member/singer is getting experience for singing and the audience will notice the excellent musicianship and forget about the vocals they heard. Since this singer sung in the last set, it's not going to make or break the audience's opinion of the band.

Trying out a new song at a gig

If you are not sure a certain song will go over well, sandwich that song between two hot numbers. For example: Perform a hot song you know everyone will like, then put the questionable song next, then another hot number that everyone loves. This way, if the questionable song bombs, the audience won't have that much of a memory of it, since two hot songs were next to it.

Should you have a "main showperson" on stage?

It's great to have someone up there to announce the band and chat with the audience. Many times we have not had anyone in our band who wanted to play that role. Mostly, we played tune after tune without saying too much to the audience, and our band still got asked back for another gig. Now, if you have one or two people who want to play the front person role, try them both out at the same gig on different sets, or try one at one gig, and the other at another gig.

Be a duo or trio if certain band members can't make a gig

Sometimes gigs will come up that not everyone can make, nor can you find replacements for some band members. You have to let the band know that you will go out as a duo or trio if some band members are willing to do this.

For example: Our bass player and drummer could not make a gig. So my husband played left-hand piano bass and we brought a drum machine to the gig. Our guitarist showed up and we all sang, too. The gig went over very well. We prefer to have a full band, but we won't pass up trio gigs.

Deciding on a band name

You should all come up with a name you can love, but if you just can't think of a name everyone agrees on, the leader should pick a name and go with it until you find something better. Since the leader started the band, and because band members can come and go, the leader will have to live with the band name for a long time if his band becomes known. So, he should have the final say. As for registering your band name to prevent others from using it, I believe you only have to do so if your band becomes nationally known. Until then, if you feel that no one in the locations in which you perform has the same band name, don't bother with the registration process. If you want to register the band name anyway, research "registering a band name" on google. There are some sites that are free and give you some sort of registration/protection of your band name. I don't believe it's the real thing unless you register with the big sites, whom you have to pay to secure a band name. I registered our band under the free band sites.

SECTION 3

Where the gigs are
and how to get them

Where the gigs are

Clubs: There are clubs for all age groups, from teenagers to 50-year-olds and up. A listing in the local newspaper usually lists all the clubs and the styles of music they hire. You can also research clubs in your area on the internet. A lot of clubs may want you to play until 1:00 or 2:00 AM, so make sure your musicians want to do this.

Lodges: Most older age groups play at the dinner dances at The American Legions, VFW Lodges, Moose Lodges and Elks Lodges. They have many, many, dinner dances and usually look for country or oldies (40s/50s) music.

The people are very nice and will often hire you right over the phone. Often, you only need to send a flyer/cassette/business card to them to get hired. And they will call you instead of you calling them. I say "cassette" because a lot of older folks don't have CD players as yet. It's true. The internet has all the addresses/phone numbers of these lodges, which are located everywhere in the USA. They have fun, appreciative audiences and the shows generally are from 7:00 to 10:00 PM, although some lodges run 8:00 PM to midnight. We love these gigs!

Swap meets: You often play out in the hot sun or cold weather during the daytime. We've had band members who refused to play in the heat. Swap meets attract all age groups, so you may not have the certain appreciative age group sitting there all day watching you. Sure, some other age groups can appreciate your music, but some won't give a hoot!

Fairs: Some fairs only pay top acts, and other bands play for free. Like swap meets, a variety of age groups attend.

You may have gaps with no one watching the band and then time spans where you are appreciated.

Senior centers: Yes, a lot of them do pay, and some pay pretty well. These are the rewarding gigs and the audiences appreciate any type of music as long as it is not heavy metal or rap. You know what I mean. They normally go for 40s/50s music of any style. The gigs are usually early afternoon or very early evenings. We love these gigs!

Hospitals: Some do pay you, but not much. If it is a convalescent hospital for seniors, the music should be 40s/50s style. If it is a regular hospital, I'd stick with the easy listening in country, pop, jazz, or standards from any style of music.

Casinos: 50s/60s/70s music goes over well here. It depends on the age group that frequents the casino room the band is in. You might have to play till midnight or longer, but not always.

Churches: If it is a senior church dance or a youth group dance, play the style of music that fits the age of the audience. Most often, early evening gigs here.

Restaurants/bistros: Music from the 40s to 70s are in these places, anything from oldies to jazz to easy listening. Usually early evening shows at these venues, but some stay open much later than others do.

50th wedding anniversaries: Most of the crowd consists of the senior couple being honored and their senior friends, but there could be loads of children and grandkids there, too. Have a mixed bag of music from all eras prepared, or better yet, ask the couple giving the party what age group will be there. Ask if you can prepare any special songs for them. Usually, the seniors will leave the gig by 10:00 PM or sooner, but their kids/grandkids may stay till midnight; that's why you need music for that generation, too.

Weddings: Depends on the age group of who is getting married and how many different age groups will be in the audience. Try to give something to everyone. Ask what age groups will be there and ask if there are any special songs they may want to hear. Weddings can be afternoons and early evenings.

Resorts: These places pay a lot but sometimes the stage is tiny. You would think that a huge resort with golf courses, horseback riding, swimming pools and the like would have a huge stage, but sometimes these places have a tiny ol' stage and it's hard to cram even four band members on it. I'm not saying every resort has a tiny stage, but it was just sort of funny to see this at the resort we played at. Our gigs ran from 8:00 PM to midnight and the pay was very good.

Showcases for original music: Yes, these do exist, but not as much anymore. The internet or local newspaper should have the scoop on what places showcase original music. A lot of high-profile places make you pay to play there, so watch out for this. They may also give you all or some of the pay from the door (from people who paid to get in to see the band).

Note: If you are not sure the place allows smoking :
No one in my band smokes, and I don't want to book gigs at places that allow smoking. So many places break the law on this; you really have to call and find out. I usually call earlier in the week, without identifying myself, and ask what kind of music they have there and if they allow smoking.

Someone might say, "We all smoke here even though the law says not to." They could also tell you that smoking is in designated areas only and not near the stage. We were told there was no smoking at a gig, only to find the place full of smoke when we got there. But I had brought my fan, which diverts smoke away from the stage if you angle it right; plus, we opened up the back door behind the stage, and that solved the problem.

Getting gigs by phone calling

- I ask to talk to whoever books bands.

- I introduce myself and the band and talk about the style of music we perform and how it would fit into their venue.

- I tell the manager how many musicians he will have on stage, who sings, and what instruments they play. Managers love to hear that they are getting a lot of singers or instruments.

- I give the names of some of the top artists and song titles we perform. Give both, because sometimes they remember the artist, not the song, or vice versa.

- I mention we do take requests.

- I tell the manager that if he wants certain songs performed for an event, to let us know what those songs are so the band can have them prepared for the show.

- I mention a lot of the places we've played and how long the band has been together (even if there were changes of players, the band was still together for a certain number of years, with a few of the original players). If you haven't played at a bunch of places or had the band together that long, skip saying any of this. Do mention that everyone loves your band, because I am sure you had people hear your band, even if it was only at rehearsal.

- I am frequently asked what I charge. I start at a basic ballpark dollar amount I think the place can afford, and then see if that works. If it sounds outrageous to the manager, I lower it and see if we can come to an agreement. Sometimes I will say that this time, I can play for lower than I normally charge but if they really like us and would want us back, I would probably raise the price next time. They tend to think that is fair.

What will happen next is that you could be booked over the phone and asked to send a gig contract. Or you won't be booked but asked to send a promo pak with a CD (or cassette) so they can read/listen to the band first. Ask how detailed of a promo pak they want, because most of the time all they need is a business card and flyer to keep on hand until a gig crops up. Again, a lot of older folks want a cassette and don't have CD players; ask if they want a cassette or CD sent along with the flyer and business card.

You can negotiate the free food/drinks/rooms you may be able to get, either over the phone or you can put this request in the gig contract. Have the manager check the boxes as to how much food/drinks or free rooms (like at a hotel) may be included.

Ask what time the doors will be open for you to set up. You need to put this info in the contract the manager signs. You need to let him know how much time you need to set up, because someone has to be there to let you in. Don't assume someone will be there. Get the facts.

Ask who is responsible for paying the band and at what time to get the money. This is important. At some gigs, they pay the band an hour before the band is finished. At a resort and swap meet we played at, we were told to get our pay an hour before the gig ended. Once, I forgot to do this, and the person who was to pay me had almost left to go home. Don't expect anyone to remember to pay you; you have to go to them. Also, find out who (get a name) is to pay you. Nothing worse than trying to find out who is going to pay you at the gig and none of the employees know. You can waste an hour trying to find who is to pay you. Don't let this happen.

Ask if there will be a band table you can sit at during breaks.

Even though you are getting paid, you may want to bring a tip jar or two, and ask if this okay. Some places don't allow it.

If you want to bring friends/family members to sit at your band table, ask if this is okay. They may have to pay for a cover charge or for food, so don't assume they get in for free.

Ask if the place puts out a newsletter in which your band will be advertised and if you can get a copy of it for your promo pak. People who look through promo paks like to see these types of things.

Other ways to get gigs

Mail a flyer and business card to a place you want to play
This approach seems to work well for our band and we have booked a lot of gigs this way. Owners/managers do keep our flyer/business card and have called us for gigs.

You can also follow up with a phone call if you want to make sure they received what you sent them. On the internet, you can research restaurants, clubs in your area to play at, or type in a specific lodge's name (e.g. "Elks Lodge") and all the lodges in that area will come up.

Talk to the owner/manager (in person) where you want to play
It's best to call first and see if the owner/manager can allow a few minutes to talk to you. Bring your promo pak/CD and explain a little bit about who you are, what type of music you play, and where you have performed.

Put flyers on cars who may hire you for private parties
Just thought I'd throw this one in, although we've never done it.

Put an advertisement in:
Newspapers
Put ads in wealthy areas' newspapers if you want gigs that pay well.

The internet

There are places to advertise your band on the internet. Soundclick.com lets you upload your tunes and more. Or type in www.google.com and research "band advertising."

Senior magazines/newsletters

This has worked for us in getting calls for gigs. Placing an ad in these magazines/newsletters usually costs less than $10 if you keep the wording minimal.

Club magazines/newsletters

Never tried this, but other bands have put band ads in the various club magazines/newsletters they belong to and have had a lot of success getting gigs. Try putting ads in areas where the rich live and you'll get higher-paying gigs.

Local cable TV

We have been on our local cable TV music programs a few times. Check with the local cable TV in your area and see if they allow bands. It was free for us to be on TV.

Do free fairs

Some fairs pay and some don't. If you play a free fair, have lots of flyers and business cards around, plus a tip jar. You'd be surprised, but gigs do come out of doing free shows. We played a free fair and the mayor was in the crowd and hired us for many good paying gigs.

Do some free gigs at a restaurant or some clubs, etc.
You can offer to do a free gig at a place that does not have music, to see if they would want it. Have your tip jar, flyers, and business cards out and see what happens. A lot of restaurants will give you free food, too, so ask about this.

Play the dinner hour before the big acts come on
You can offer to bring your band in to play for happy hour, for free, for a small fee, or for food/drinks only, and see if the managers like you. They may decide to hire your band permanently for the dinner hour or may use you as the main act. Make sure you have your tip jar, flyers, and business cards out.

College radio can play your band's cover or original tunes
Send a promo pak/CD to college radio and see if they will play it or announce where your band is playing.

Internet band promotions, TV, and radio

SirLinksalot.net gives a list of shows that need talent. Choose the "casting calls" link from the homepage. This will take you to a page that tells you what big TV shows are coming to your town and what sort of musical talent they may be looking for. TV Rules.net is a similar site.

You can download the application forms from most of the sites. Other sites recommend mailing one short audition tape and picture, describing what sets you apart from others. I've read that every tape gets listened to.

RealityAuditions.com allows you to complete a personal web page with two photos and a detailed bio. Casting directors for music or acting browse these sites and 150 executives browse them daily. A year's membership costs around $30.

Books to buy

The Musician's Atlas

With names and addresses of places nationwide, this book has everything: thousands of music industry contacts, film and TV music, publishers, commercial and college radio, record stores and distributors, showcase venues, clubs, recording studios, music lawyers, and booking agents.

The Indie Bible

Four thousand publications that review CD's, and 3,200 radio stations that accept CD's for possible airing.

How to Promote Your Music Successfully on the Internet
by David Nevue

This book is the "real thing"...no joke. It's got everything you need to know about music marketing on the internet, radio, etc. Check it out at www.promoteyourmusic.com!

If you want a booking agent
to book your band

Castinglist.com/showbizltd.com (booking agents)

This link will give you the most up-to-date information of every booking agent in your area for a fee of $15.00. They give you names and addresses of legitimate places that are seeking talent at the moment. They only list licensed companies that don't ask for a fee upfront. This company will send you updates every time a listing goes out of business or a new listing is added. I highly recommend getting this list. Pay $19.00 and they will send you typed labels for the list. They send the lists or labels out within two business days.

Ask at the places you perform if they ever use a booking agent to find bands. If they say yes, ask them who they use and get the phone number. You'd be surprised how many of these numbers are not listed in the phone book or on the internet, so make sure you get the phone number and not just the name of the place.

You can try to find booking agents on the internet, but most of them I called were out of business. You could ask other bands who they use as a booking agent, but most won't tell you who they use, especially if you do the same style of music they do. They feel you are competition for them for the same gigs.

What to put in a flyer or promo pak

If you are going after high-profile, huge-paying gigs in Vegas or showcase events in Hollywood, then, yeah, you need a super professional CD and promo pak of pictures, bio, song lists, etc. We don't cover that in this book.

We cover the mainstream gigs that do not require much expense in terms of a promo pak. Most of the promo material we send out we make on our own computer. We also recorded and made the CD of the band at home.

Note: Some places will book you even if you never send a CD or cassette to them. They feel the flyer/reading material is believable and will book you.

My promo pak that gets gigs

Introductory letter

This letter should include: An introduction of yourself, your band's name, and what style of music you perform. List some of the artists and song titles you cover (You need to list both because some people may not remember the artist and some may not remember the title; cover yourself and have them both down). Give a mini-bio on the musicians; who plays what instrument and who sings. Add a short blurb on the many places you have played such as fairs, country clubs, etc. and be sure to include in the pak an attachment which lists everywhere you have played in the past few years. If you don't have tons of places you have played, then just list some places you have played in the letter. If you don't have any places to mention yet, then just share with them that everyone who hears your band loves it! Be sure to include compliments you have received such as, "People say the band is the best they have heard since..." Make sure you have included your address and phone number so they can easily contact you.

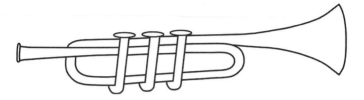

CD or cassette

A lot of lodges that cater to people over 50 years old want a cassette, but most other places would want a CD. We made our CDs at home. If your band members change a lot, you don't have to keep re-doing the CD with the new band members. As long as your sound is basically the same, send whatever CD you made previously. Now, if the players you currently have can't live up to what is on that CD, either change the players or make a new CD. You have to be honest about what sound a place is going to get from your band.

Band picture

If some of the musicians have changed and you have not taken a recent band picture, use the old picture. You can list below the picture that the drummer/bass player etc. has changed, and put in the new names of the people who took their place.

Band bio on each musician

Even if they don't have much of a bio, you can still put descriptive terminology such as, "Dynamic vocals and superb guitar playing makes Don the most talked-about musician in the Antelope Valley." Something like that, as long as you feel it is a true statement.

Written articles on the band

If your band was written up in a newsletter/newspaper etc., put that in, too.

Song list of everything you perform

List includes song titles and the original artists who sang them. You need to put both, because some people will not remember the song title unless they see the artist, and some won't remember the artist unless they see the song title. Have both to cover yourself.

Places you have played

I include the past few years' worth. If you haven't played that many places, then list a few. For example, "Performed at private parties, fairs, car shows, lodges and much more"—and don't put the time periods in! Maybe by the time they read your promo, you will have been booked at other places. Let's hope.

Send an SASE (self-addressed stamped envelope) with the music contract so they can mail the original back to you. They keep the copy. You need to buy some carbon paper for this. (See the sample of the music gig contract.)

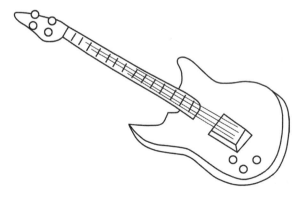

Sample of gig contract

THE BABYBOOMERS BAND
Music Contract

DATE OF PERFORMANCE: July 11, 2004

PLACE OF PERFORMANCE: Elks Lodge, 5588 Sierra Hwy.
Santa Monica, CA 91405

TIME OF PERFORMANCE: 6:30 pm – 10:30 pm

SET-UP TIME: 5:30 pm (so they have the doors open for us to get in)

PAY FOR PEFORMANCE: $400.00
CASH PREFERRED

If Not Paid in Cash Make Check Out To: 'John Taylor'
(NOTE: Don't have them make the check out to the band's name, because no bank will cash it unless you are registered as a dba at City Hall)

Deposit of : $ _____
(they will fill this out if they give a deposit)

Free Food/Drinks for Band: yes ( ), no ( )

SIGNATURE OF BAND MEMBER:

_____

SIGNATURE OF PERSON HIRING BAND:

_____

Any Questions Call John at (818) 111-3333

SECTION 4

Before the gig, situations at the gig,
money issues and getting paid,
after the gig

Call or email your band members the day before the gig

You'd be surprised about how many musicians forget the day, time, and place of the gig, even if you've already given them the information in person or via email, or told them on the phone. You need to remind them of these things as well as the following:

- The pay of the gig. We've had musicians argue that the pay was not what I had told them they were going to get. This is why we keep a copy of all emails we send to band members about the pay, and call them about it the day before the gig.

- Who had previously agreed to play overtime and how much you would charge for that.

- What they need to wear on stage. Some gigs require fancy clothes so it's important to remind the musicians of this.

- Loudness level your band will play at. If you are playing a small coffee shop, you are probably not going to be blasting the music. Sure, you can tell a band member at the gig to stop doing that if he starts it up, but it's best to tell him before the gig, to avoid getting into a huge argument on stage. On one occasion, our drummer kept playing increasingly louder and louder. He argued with us, on stage, that he felt it was appropriate to play loudly. I asked the manager what he thought of the sound level, and sure enough, he said, "Turn it down."

If the band gets free food and drinks all night, let them

know so they don't have to hassle with packing food or buying food on breaks somewhere.

Remind them to bring things such as charts, lyrics, any lights, etc. You may not have to remind all the musicians, only the ones who have a habit of forgetting these things.

Now, if you really think your musicians are totally responsible and you don't have to check up on them like this, fine. That's great! More power to ya!

You can also call the place you are going to play the day before the gig or the day of the gig

You need to make sure the doors will be opened at the time you are to set up. You don't want to arrive there and find out you have to wait outside for an hour until someone comes to open the door.

You need to confirm that your band is playing there, because sometimes whoever books the gig makes a mistake. You may arrive at the gig and there is another band in your place.

If you recently fired a band member, he may call to try to cancel your next gig. Yes, this has happened to us. It is a good idea to call the gig to make sure it's still "on."

Note: If your intuition tells you not to call the gig and everything will be fine, then great, go with what your gut tells you.

What if a band member does not dress correctly?

We had a fancy gig and a band member showed up in jeans (bad, greasy jeans, I might add). He was told two weeks before the gig what to wear. I didn't think I'd have to call him the day of the gig to remind him, but apparently I should have. It was kind of embarrassing, but thank God the music was good enough to counter-act this.

Bring extra lyrics, set lists charts, in case they forget theirs

We have a typed list of the items we need to bring to a gig and we go through the list to make sure we are not forgetting anything. We bring extra lyrics and charts in case someone in the band forgets theirs. Here are some of the things I put on my checklist.

- Lyrics
- Charts
- Food, water
- Video camera and/or regular camera
- Cell phone
- A fan, in case there is smoking and I need to blow the smoke from the stage
- Sometimes I bring a drum machine in case our drummer has an emergency.
- All of the instruments we play, including microphones, PA system.
- Sometimes audience members love to use our percussion instruments, such as the tambourine and maracas.
- My own chair or stool. Some gigs run short on these so I always bring my own to use on stage.
- The gig contract
- A blank gig contract

- Two tip jars with two TV trays to put them on. You will want to put one tip jar by the stage and one tip jar by the bar. Each tip jar should be labeled "Band Tips."
- Duct tape. Parts of instruments have been known to break off suddenly and duct tape comes in handy. It can be used for many weird little things that can crop up.
- Extension cords and electrical outlet adapters. Sometimes there are not enough outlets to plug equipment into so you need to bring adapters and extension cords.

Bring extra percussion instruments for the audience to use

A member of the audience came up to our band and asked if she could borrow the tambourine. We were not using it right then, so I gave it to her. She started to dance while she played the tambourine and the audience loved it. They got up and danced with her. The tips we got were tremendous. Now I bring extra percussion instruments to each gig.

Bring the gig contract they signed, in case they say they never booked you there

Yes, this has happened to us, three times!!! Once at a resort, once at a casino, and once at a lodge gig. The resort actually called before the gig and said not to come because they had a mix-up in booking but they mailed a check that did clear the bank for us. Then at a casino, we all showed up that night to play the gig, and we saw a karaoke party arriving. The manager paid us and said that someone had booked a karaoke party in there and they didn't know our band would be there that night. At the lodge, our band showed up and the manager said no one ever booked us and that they were going to listen to the radio and drink all night. I had the contract with me and it was signed by him, so he had to pay. It wasn't that easy to get the money, but with the contract in hand, what else could the lodge do? It actually took me a couple of days to get all the cash, and I had to keep hounding them for it.

Bring an extra blank gig contract

The place where you are performing may ask you back or someone from the audience can come up and want to book the band for a gig. With an extra blank contract or two on hand, you can have them sign it. Make sure to bring the carbon paper so they can keep a copy. This solidifies the deal right then and there. If you don't have the blank contract with you, you take your chances that they will change their mind and not call you.

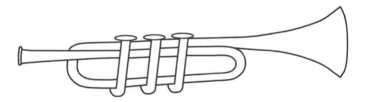

Bring a cassette or video recorder to the gig

You simply must bring either a cassette recorder or video recorder to the gig, because when you discuss the problems of the gig at your next rehearsal, all the proof of what happened is right there. This will save a lot of "I never played it that way" issues. Plus, it will capture the exceptional band moments and you will have wonderful memories of the night.

Set up time should be an hour before the gig

The standard rule for most bands is that set-up time is an hour before the gig. Some band members may think that it only takes minutes for them to set up their equipment, but you can usually expect the unexpected. You may have to spend time trying to find outlets to plug the equipment into, managers and audience members talking to you, the stage might be too small for all of the equipment to fit onto, and dealing with 'who stands where on stage' issues. Don't rush in at the last minute and try to set up your equipment. There are usually interruptions of some kind.

Should you help band members unload their equipment?

I know this is a nice helpful idea and if you want to do it you can. But remember, if you bang their equipment on something or even scratch it, you may never hear the end of it and you may have to pay for it. Also, your back may be sore just from unloading your own equipment. When in doubt, unload your own stuff and let the others do likewise.

Unload the equipment in gig clothes or street clothes?

Most musicians will dress in street clothes (jeans) while unloading their equipment at the gig and then change into their gig clothes once their equipment is set up. If the audience is already inside eating and the manager looks at you in a strange way about how you are dressed, explain that you change into your performance clothes once you have set up the equipment. Now, if the gig allows jeans, set up and perform in them!

Set out the two tips jars and CDs you want to sell

We bring two tip jars and two TV trays and put one tip jar by the stage and one at the bar. These tip jars are labeled "Band Tips" to keep them separate from wait staff tips. We also put our CDs we sell near the stage tip jar, so that we can keep an eye on them.

If another band plays before you and won't get off stage

Certain places, like fairs, will hire a different band to play every hour or so. You may find that you show up to play the fair gig and the band before you is still playing and won't get off the stage. They may claim they have another hour or so to play. If you have your contract with you, you can prove that your band was hired for a certain timeslot. You need to have a contract signed even for free fair gigs. If by some strange coincidence they, too, have a contract for the same time and the manager overbooked the place, you'd have to locate the manager. If you can't reach him, come to some understanding with the band on stage and try to divide the time.

You find out that bands are backed up to play due to sound and equipment problems

Here is another situation: Many bands are lined up to play at a benefit or a fair situation. For example, our band showed up on time to play, only to find out that the bands were backed up about four hours behind schedule because of the sound equipment breaking down. The persons who ran the event were also cutting back on how much time each band could play. It was 105 degrees out and we didn't feel like waiting around for four hours. This was a free gig, as well. Before we left, we asked the band that was performing on stage at the time if some of our band members could perform with them, which they agreed to. They were more than happy to have a trumpet player to add to their sound and also a great singer we gave them. At least we got something out of the experience and some of us got to perform.

Band members who show up late to set up

Most bands show up one hour before the gig to set up. If a band member shows up at the last minute, he cannot choose where he wants to be on stage. Hopefully, he will have a good reason for being late because it looks bad for the audience to see someone frantically setting up at the last minute. Don't get into too big of a discussion right then. Just set up and start on time. You can discuss his situation at break or the next day.

If band members don't like the gig and leave

You wouldn't think anyone would stoop to this, but it has happened. I tell my band that the places we play are classy or are dives. But because I haven't been to all them personally, we all take our chances on what the gig will be like when we get there. Two band members once thought a gig they arrived at was beneath them and took their PA and left the rest of us. I should have brought my extra PA, but who would have ever thought this could have happened? I won't even get into the firing of these people, nor how we handled the pay and the rest of the night. I'll save that for another book!

Who stands "where" on stage

Each stage is different and until all band members arrive it's hard to say where each person will stand. Now, if the band members do not all show up at the same time, whoever gets there first gets to be where he wants to be. You can't re-arrange everything you set up if a late band member shows up and wants it all changed. Unless you think his idea is great and have time to change it all around, leave it be. Hey, he shouldn't have been late, so you don't have to change anything. First come, first served. All stages are different; you cannot pre-decide who stands where.

Setting up on stage and talking too loud through mics

If you are on stage talking to each other while setting up your equipment, don't stand near the microphone if it is turned on, or the whole audience will hear everything you are saying. Yes, this has happened to us.

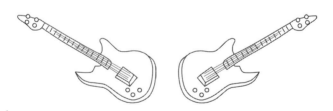

Take band pictures at break if you can

At the first break, when everyone is aglow from playing the first set, snap a band picture if you can. Before the gig starts, everyone is racing about to set up, and after the gig ends, everyone wants to go home. If you can, catch the musicians at break time before they eat/drink etc., and snap a picture.

No mini-gigs (before the gig or on breaks) unless asked

We had two band members who, without asking, did their own mini-gig with a totally different style of music than what our band plays. Before our gig started, they started to play/sing music from a different era, without asking if this was okay with the managers or the band members.

At breaks, some band members want to sing whatever they want to sing. If you don't mind having this happen, fine. But they should really ask before they up and sing their own stuff, don't ya think?

Don't let the band members warm up with songs that have nothing to do with the style of music you are going to play

We have had band members warming up on stage playing an entirely different style of music than what we were going to play. The people in the audience, though eating and chatting, could still hear the warm-up music and probably thought this was the type of music they were going to hear all night. Tell your band members to warm up with songs you will actually be playing, so if anyone hears, they know the style of music they will be hearing that night. In addition, the audience gets in the mood for the style of music to be performed. We once had someone warming up with heavy metal tunes at a senior gig!

What if the whole band arrives late because they got the time mixed up?

If the leader gave everyone the wrong info on what time to show up, have the band play overtime to make up for it. For example, if the band should have been playing from 7:00 to 11:00 PM but started at 7:30, then play till 11:30.

Band member can't make it to the gig and finds a replacement at the last minute

Well, if he has a good excuse and found a decent replacement, fine. But if the excuse was lame and so was the replacement, you need to talk with the band member about this.

Band member canceled your gig, took another gig

A member of your band may get tempted to take another gig that pays a lot more. He does not tell you the real reason, but instead:

- pulls a no-show
- calls at the last minute and says he's sick
- calls a month before to let you find a sub for him, but doesn't tell you the real reason he is canceling
- calls a month before and has a sub for you (but doesn't tell you he took another gig)

We tell our musicians that if they get a huge-paying gig with another band once in a while, to let us know. We are not going to stop them from taking a gig that pays $500 per man. But if this musician continuously takes gigs with other bands, we consider him a sub in our band and find someone more permanent. What I am saying is that our musicians should not have to lie about taking a huge-paying gig with another band.

Now, if the musician takes a gig with another band for the same night your band is to play, and he does it to "try this band out" and it isn't for any more pay than what you'd pay him, this seems dishonest to me. He shouldn't be trying out another band on a committed gig date with your band.

The gig has smoke and told you there was no smoking

Bring a fan with you on stage. You can divert some of the air out the doors. Ask if you can keep a door or window open near you.

Bring friends who dance to the gig

One of our band members brought a friend who likes to dance, either dancing alone or with someone in the audience. This was good because it loosened up the crowd to get up there and dance. You should ask if friends are allowed to come to the gig.

Performing while reading charts/lyrics or have them memorized?

Most casual dance gigs won't notice if you are performing while reading your charts or lyrics. The lyrics can be strategically placed in such a way that no one will notice you are reading them while singing. You can place them off to the side on speakers or down below on an amp. Drummers can clip lyrics on various parts of the drum set such that no one in the audience can tell that they're reading the lyrics while singing.

Naturally, it looks a lot better if you can have at least the front show persons memorize some of these things so they can look out and play and sing to the audience. That is the ideal to strive for in every band.

Following the set list or not

Strictly following a set list or not should have been discussed at rehearsal. You may get to a gig and the people are still eating dinner; the manager asks if you could only play slow songs for the first hour. Naturally, you cannot follow the set list if the set list had a bunch of fast songs upfront. Also, at some gigs, the audience can request to hear more slow or fast tunes, so you may have to jump around the set list. If the musicians have their lyrics/charts in alphabetical order, this shouldn't be a problem. Flip to the tune in alphabetical order. If they have these tunes in set order, however, it could take some time to locate the songs. One solution would be for the musicians to have two booklets with them: one with the tunes in alphabetical order and one with the tunes in set order. Sounds like a hassle but it can save lag time on stage.

Don't put a song you don't know that well in the first set

I'll never forget the lesson I learned when I really wanted a song I sing put in the first set, even though I knew the band had only rehearsed it twice. I had invited a friend I hadn't seen in many years (and who had never heard me sing) to come to this gig. The song started out fine; then, one of the band members kept playing the verse when the chorus should have been started. The song was a mess. Unless you feel that your musicians really know a song well, don't put a questionable song in the first set. The first two sets are when people really judge your band.

Make sure your first two sets have many of the good songs in them

Most people judge your band by the first and second sets. I'd make sure to put plenty of your hot tunes in these sets. Even though the audience may be eating during the first set of a dance gig, they are still listening to your band. You may think, "Well, if they are eating, my band should play slow songs for the whole first set." Don't do this either,because we had audience members come up to us and say, "Is this what we are going to be getting the rest of the night—slow songs?" Some audience members will actually get up from the dinner table and dance if they hear a song they like. We suggest you play a mixed bag of fast and slow songs while the audience is eating.

Situations at the gig while performing

Lag time between songs

Whether you have your songs in set order (if you plan to rigidly follow a set list) or in alphabetical order (so you can flip easily to whatever song is called out) should have been discussed at rehearsal. There is nothing worse than having lag time on stage waiting for someone to find a song. If you are real savvy, each person can have their charts/lyrics in alphabetical order and in set order.

Have someone from the audience sing one song with the band

Seeing one of "their own" singing up on stage totally loosens up the audience. It won't turn into a karaoke night, so don't worry about that. The audience will feel like you are relating to them, that you like them. They'll be much more open to your songs. Now, if a gig just doesn't feel right to do this at, then don't. We don't do this at every gig.

Having friends you know "sit in" (meaning they play/sing, too)

Many bands bring their friends or family to "sit in" at a gig—singing or playing a few tunes with your band, even though they are not in the band. These folks can help make your band look and sound good. We usually pay our sit-ins something for coming to the show. A lot of bands feel these people get exposure and don't need to be paid. It's up to you. You can have sit-ins sing or play all night if you want. Discuss it with them: how much they want to do and for what pay, if any. We've had singers sing with us and sax/trombonists add their specialty. Normally, our band only consists of guitar/bass/drums/piano/trumpet, but with a sit-in who can play sax or trombone, we really sound hot!

If someone either plays too loud or too soft

If you feel a band member is playing too loud or soft, you will have to confront him. If he fixes the volume and then turns it back to where he wanted it, you will have to confront him again. If he won't take direction from you, confront the whole band and get them behind you to get him to comply.

If this band member is drunk and will not do what you say, insisting on playing it to the level he wants or picking a fight on stage, ask the manager of the place what he thinks. If he agrees with you, have him confront the band member. You gotta do what you gotta do.

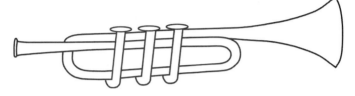

If there is a fight on stage between band members

We've had one band member tell another, between songs, that he was not playing the songs the way we rehearsed them. A loud fight ensued. The audience could hear the loudness of it but could not make out the words. I then spoke up and said, "Oh, we seem to have had an emergency!!! Please bear with us while we handle this." We decided we would discuss the matter outside at break time, which we did. The gig did continue and they even asked us to stay overtime and paid us, but it was still embarrassing that the fight did happen. Yes, we do have the fight on videotape.

If a band member is rude to the audience

We had a band member tell off someone who was asking for a request—it was his birthday and he wanted to hear a special song. The band member hates when people ask for requests and told the man off, saying, "You can't expect us to know everything" etc. etc. etc. Horrified after hearing this, we apologized to this man and told him that the band member had a hard day. We were never asked back to this place and eventually let the band member go, due to his drug and drinking habits. He also showed up late a lot.

If the tune is played wrong but the singer sings it right

I was singing a song and one of the band members was playing it totally wrong. I kept singing, hoping he would figure it out. He didn't, but what can you do? I couldn't guess what he was going to do and follow him, so I kept singing the tune the way it should have been sung. Yeah, it was embarrassing, but people clapped. Maybe they thought the song was supposed to go that way, who knows?

If the tune is played right and the singer sings it wrong

This has happened. I was singing the verse section when the chorus was being played by the band. All I could do was try to follow along with the music I heard and stop singing for a moment to hear what the band was actually playing. Eventually, I got back on track, singing it right.

Band member walks off stage in middle of performance

We had a band member walk off stage and go outside. He was so pissed that another band member was monopolizing the whole show, he said it was best he go outside rather than make a scene on stage. After talking to him on break time, we told him to go back on stage and finish the show. We would talk to the "monopolizer," which we tried to do. He wouldn't listen to us. In order not to provoke a huge fight on stage, we had to let him do his ego thing. We spoke with him the next day in depth about how it wasn't right that he took over the show. It was all on videotape, so when he denied it, we played the video.

When a band member is drunk
on stage and it shows

You've got to put the drunken musician in the background on stage. Have other band members stand in front of him and play. Another tactic is to tell the drunk to go behind the stage and rest/sober up; the remaining band members can carry the show without him (hopefully). If he won't go behind stage and is unruly with band members, take a mini-break and at least get him off the stage.

Joking on stage to the audience
and it doesn't work

If a band member is telling jokes onstage between songs and the audience is not laughing, he should know to stop telling the jokes. If he doesn't get the hint, the leader will have to tell him that the band is going to start the music. Or, just start the music up so he stops.

When a band member is flirting too
much offstage and embarrassing
the manager and others

Some managers do not like intense sexual flirting with their audience, either onstage or on breaks. They won't hire the band back if they see someone monopolizing their members of the opposite sex, especially in a debasing/degrading sort of way. Sure, it is okay to meet people, when handled in a more subdued manner. If someone in your band is outrageously flirting and making a fool out of himself, you have to divert the band member's attention to some band issues. If you have no band issues, divert his attention toward what you thought of his performance (good or bad); just divert him away from a potentially embarrassing situation!

Finding band members when break time is up and getting them back on stage

Break time is over and it's time for the band to get back up on stage. Problem is, you can't locate them. You can start to warm up on stage by playing a tune to see if they hear it. Or you will have to literally go and find them. We once found all our band members eating at a table. They really wanted to finish their food and take a longer break. They said that no one would notice or care. You'd be surprised how many people (managers and the audience) do notice and do care and want the band back on stage. I've even had an audience member come up to me and ask, "Is the band coming back on stage soon?" So yes, they do notice.

How to handle requests

Hey, if you know the song, play it. If you don't know it or are not sure your band members have ever played it, do this:

Get out a fake book of songs (a book of charts to read from) and see if you can muddle your way through it. If the band starts to play it and it sounds terrible, cut the song short. We tried to play this waltz all the way through and got criticized for doing it instead of being praised for at least trying to do it. If you can play the song pretty decently, then do that. Sometimes the requester will be grateful that you tried and will tip you nicely for it.

If you don't know the song, say, "We don't know that one but we know something similar" and then name the song you know. Or say, "Here is a copy of the songs we do know. Maybe you may want to hear one of these songs." (Make sure you have an extra copy.) Or have them write down the request on a napkin and say, "If we know this, we will play it for you soon."

Should you announce you have a tip jar?

A band member of ours suddenly announced on stage that we had a tip jar and that people could help support the musicians, etc. At the place we were playing, no one seemed to mind this, but at another place they hated it and thought it was tacky. Take your chances on whether it's the right thing to do.

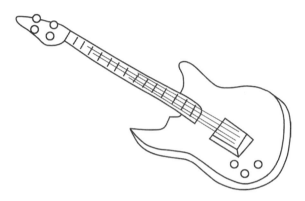

Playing an original tune at a cover gig

We have performed some original tunes we wrote and other band members wrote. They fit the style of the gig and the audience loved it, so it was okay to try those out. You can even announce you have an original CD for sale, which the audience can buy at the breaks.

Announcing you have CDs to sell

You can announce you have CDs for sale, whether they are cover material CDs or original music. You may want to have some free cookies at the table and say, "Free cookies at the CD sale table"; that will at least get them to go over there. Bring a colorful tray or table with a colorful piece of cloth on it, to lure people over. Announce you will autograph the CDs.

Money Issues and Getting Paid

If someone asks a band member how much you charge, direct them to the leader of the band

Don't let any of the band members book a gig or give out information on how much you charge. The leader usually doesn't book all the gigs for the same hours or price. Each gig is different. Some allow free food/drinks and are either local or long distance gigs. Let the leader conjure up the fee for the gig.

Playing unexpected overtime and how much to charge

If the manager asks you to play overtime, you should already know which of your musicians are able to do this and how much they want for it. If not, have a quick band meeting and discuss it. Even if a few band members have to leave, sometimes the place will accept a duo or trio, just to have more music played.

Split the tips equally

We always had one tip jar for the whole band and split the money. Even if one band member was a hot player that night and people seemed to be tipping a lot on his solos, we still split the money evenly. I think once I gave that hot band member more, out of my own tip share, but the rest of the band did not like that. Discuss the issue with your band at rehearsal. I've seen bands that have tip jars for almost every band member. This seems strange to me, but if it works for them, then so be it. We usually put two tips jars out (one by the stage and one by the bar) but we split the money equally among all band members.

Getting paid by whom?

You should have asked when you booked the band if the pay would be by check or cash, who to get paid from, and when. "When" means what time do they pay the band? Some places pay the band an hour before the band finishes, so you have to remember to go get paid before the bar area that pays you closes down. If you get paid by check, you may be able to cash that check at the bar. If you don't cash the check there, be sure to inspect the check to make sure the name written on the check, the amount and the date are all correct. Don't assume it is correct even though they signed a contract that specifies who to make the check out to. Before you leave, check the check; even if you have played there before. Make sure you have the contract, because if someone says "We never agreed on that pay" you can whip out your contract. And remember, the original person who hired you may not be there; someone else may argue with you that they don't pay bands as much as your band is getting. With a signed contract to show them, you've got it all covered.

If paid in cash, count it!!!

Hey, it could be wrong, so count it right away. And count it right in front of whoever pays you. This is important because it could be wrong. Don't let over-excitement, being too tired or in a rush to pack up and go home stop you from counting this cash. Sometimes the person who pays the cash is paying you the sum that they pay other bands and it may not be what is in your contract. The original person who hired you may not be there. Hopefully, you have your signed contract with you, too.

If you feel the check is going to bounce, cash it right away

We played a really nice restaurant with an owner who also had a high-ranking government job, but we felt like something was fishy about her cash flow. We played a few nights in a row there and each time, we had to hunt her down for a half-hour or more to get our pay, which was always by check. Something told me to cash these checks immediately, which I did. Thank God they cleared the bank, because I found out later that with another band, the check bounced and she never paid them. I felt sorry for this band since a lot of their members drove an hour to play that gig. To be ripped off like that was horrendous. Eventually, this restaurant went out of business.

Paid in counterfeit money, does it happen?

I thought I'd put this in even though it never happened to us. I was told by a member of another band that it did happen to them. So I guess that's going to be a new thing I look for when I receive cash at a gig.

Paying band members before/after the gig, if the gig pays by check

If the gig pays by check and the band members do not want to wait till the check clears the bank to get paid, you could pay them out of your own pocket after the gig—if you have it—and then keep the band check for yourself.

Naturally, you have to know that the band check is a good one and will clear the bank. Most checks from the big places don't bounce—although it has happened, not to me, but to another band I know. I would not advise paying the musicians with your cash before the gig, in case someone leaves the gig or decides, "Hey, I'm paid. I can take long breaks or don't have to try as hard on stage." I know you may not think anyone would do that, and most of the time they don't. But it's up to you to decide.

Should the musician who booked the gig get paid more?

This is between you and your band members. Sometimes it is not always the leader who books the gigs, it is another band member. Work it out between you and your band members whether you want to pay the person who books the gigs a ten percent cut off the top of the gig pay.

Should the musician who brings the PA system get paid more?

Depending on the PA a musician has, this could take an extra hour or more to set up and tear down; thus he is working longer than everyone else. If all the band members help him set it up and tear it down and carry it all out to the car, maybe you wouldn't have to pay him more. But if he has to arrive much earlier than everyone and stay later to tear it down, I'd suggest giving him something extra for that.

What if a certain musician thinks he is worth more and wants more pay?

I feel everyone in the band should get the same pay. If one of your musicians cannot make a gig and the only person you can find wants more pay than everyone else, discuss it with the band members. See if they feel hiring this person is worth it. It's best to hire someone who can accept the same pay as everyone else to avoid resentment.

Paying musicians who have been in the band longer more money, should you?

I know some bands do this, but we never have. Everyone gets the gig pay split equally. We do like to pay extra to musicians who book the gig and bring the PA system.

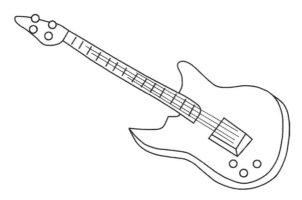

After the gig

Should you help your band members pack up their equipment after a gig?

If you play trumpet, for example, it would be so easy to leave immediately after the gig instead of helping others pack everything up for the next half-hour or so. This is entirely up to you. Remember, the person who brought the PA system may be getting paid more for staying longer to pack everything up (see previous heading this section, "Should you help band members unload their equipment?").

Keep a list of compliments you receive to put in your promo pak

Write down what happens at the gigs and keep that with your video copy. You can include these compliments in your promo pak.

It's good to keep a written mini-bio on each gig you play, in case they ask you back. That way, you will know what set list you used, what they paid, if they had free food/drinks and more.

If the band gets thrown out

If you play somewhere and they just hate the music—even though you told them the style you play—make sure you get paid if they throw you out. Have the contract and say, "We are living up to what you heard on the CD, what you read in our recommendations, and what you saw in our promo pak. If you personally don't like us, you still have to pay us."

If the band gets asked back or someone books you for a new gig somewhere else

Great! This is what you want to happen. Pull out that blank contract you should have with you and write up the deal on the spot. Make sure you have carbon paper with you so you can give them a copy.

SECTION 5

How to make a CD
from your house

Equipment you will need

Equipment that you will need to play live gigs, make a demo of your band, and make your own CDs can be simple because of the multi-functional nature of today's musical products. Fifteen years ago it would have been necessary to have a studio rig and separate live performance gear to cover all the bases as a professional musician. Today, prices have dropped tremendously on quality recording equipment, and portability has made it possible to take studio quality equipment to the gig.

For example, a Mackie DFX12 12-channel mixer is capable of satisfying live performance and studio quality recording functions for under $300. You will need a power amp of at least 200 watts to power the mixer, but the effects, such as reverb and delay, are built into the Mackie. Also, most synthesizers have built-in effects to make them sound "wet" without external reverb units. What does this mean to the average musician? It means that you no longer need to have dedicated rack spaces for sound processors and the subsequent patch cords needed to connect them to the rest of your gear. Why is less more in this case? Simple: set-up time before the gig and tear-down after the show. When you've played enough gigs over the course of the years, you come to the realization that time is indeed money. Streamlining your gear and your time spent setting up and tearing down will be a primary concern, attitudinally speaking.

A personal example that may not be all that unique is when I went into a major LA music store with a fresh new credit card ready to be maxed out with musical gear. The little components that created magic through MIDI, foot switches, and controllers were amazing to behold. Putting them all together in one or two rack boxes made the electronic musician I was becoming look formidable and super professional on stage. All the lights and knobs made it look like I knew what was happenin'. Over time, I experienced MIDI errors, sound processor errors, and sequencing software errors while playing live—usually just before a solo or during an exposed ballad accompaniment. It took me more than a few years to come to the realization that I needed to sell all my gear and get one keyboard with all the sounds I needed inside, one mixer with all the equalization and reverb built in, and one power amp to power it all. Another way I could have gone was to purchase a mixing board with its own power amp built in, saving time connecting the power amp to the mixer.

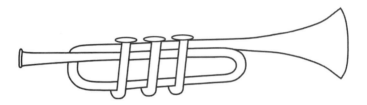

I have not regretted simplifying my live gear to make my life so much easier. Going to a gig is a much more enjoyable experience. The bottom line is that the less cords that have to be connected, the better off you will be!

A keyboard player needs a keyboard controller, with a sound module if the controller has no built-in sounds, and a power amp usually housed in a 2-6 space rack. Of course, speakers will be needed for the PA "mains" and smaller ones for at least two monitors. On smaller venues you can easily get by with just two main speakers, positioned in a way that the musicians and audience can both hear what's being performed. We don't play loud; a small room would be accommodated nicely with just a couple speakers.

Bring a lightweight yet sturdy hand truck to wheel your gear in and out of the venue. This is a must to maintain your health. I was taught by the leader of one of the groups I played in that you rarely, if ever, really pick up any piece of equipment off the ground. You simply leverage it from one place to another with the aid of a dolly or hand truck. I found this to be absolutely true. The days of carting around Hammond B3 organs are gone, but weighted action keyboard controllers and equipment racks can still be quite heavy to move around.

Recording an at-home demo can be easily accomplished by using your live performance gear described above. Your mixer, vocal microphones, and a computer with the appropriate recording and/or sequencing software will be all you need for a good home recording studio of your band.

Simply plug everything in to the mixer as if you are playing a gig but with all the band instruments going line in direct to the mixer. Next, go stereo out of the mixer and line in to your PC or Mac via the computer mini plug input. I use Adobe Audition (aka Cool Edit Pro before it was bought out) to digitally record to my hard drive. Mac users can use MOTU's Digital Performer for one example. Record, edit, and master your songs on your computer using the recording software. Lastly, use CD burning software, such as Nero or Easy CD Creator (Mac can use Toast) and burn your tunes onto a blank CD-R. You can buy CD sticky labels and use the software that comes with them to create your own CD label to apply. That's it in a nutshell on burning your own demo!

SECTION 6

How to get your songs picked up
by a music publisher, cable TV,
video CD-ROM companies,
and radio stations

Music Publishing Companies

I bought the book *The Songwriter's Market* and sent a CD out to many of these places. We had 10 songs picked between three music publishers, so the book did work for us. What you have to be aware of with music publishers is how long they will tie up your songs. This is really important! Some music publishers can tie up your songs for years and years and not do a thing with them. They wait for you to do something with the songs, and they cash in on it. Some music contracts will only tie up your songs for a year or two and if they don't do anything with the songs, you are free from the contract. This is reasonable. I feel so sorry for an acquaintance of ours who signed a contract and signed away 30 songs for 30 years!!! It has been three years so far and nothing at all has happened with her songs. Is this a horror story or what!!! Please don't do this no matter how much the publisher says he is going to push your songs. If they can't do anything within a year or two, they probably never will.

Cable TV, video, CD-ROM companies, and how they find you!

Please get your songs up on a music website such as soundclick.com. You have a great chance of someone "big" finding you. Not only have our songs been picked up by CD-ROM companies, cable TV, and video places, but also a friend of ours just had his songs picked up by a record label in a foreign country. These things do happen if you have your songs uploaded onto a music website. Some places will pay you and others will give you free software or publicity in their newsletters or in the credits. You have to work out the details. Every opportunity is different.

Performing on cable TV

Cable TV stations in many areas of the country will interview your band and let you play a song or two. This is all done for free—you don't have to pay them and they won't pay you.

Paying for a cable TV spot
to advertise your band

If you do want to pay for a commercial of your band, the rates will vary as to how much time you want and how many times a month you want it aired.

Paying for a radio spot
to advertise your band

Like the cable TV ad, it depends on how long your ad will be and how many times you have it on the air.

Getting played on the radio

Wow, it is such a thrill to hear your band on the radio, either singing a cover tune or an original tune. The Indie Bible lists 3,200 radio stations that will possibly play your CD. You can also call college radio stations in your area and ask what you need to send in (e.g. info on the band or where you are playing), along with the CD.

Getting played on internet radio

Having our songs uploaded onto many music sites brought in interest from internet radio stations that approached us and wanted permission to play our original tunes on their online radio sites. Btsradio.com, Xeradio.com, and Thestreamradio.com are a few sites to check out, or go into google.com and type in "internet radio websites" and see what comes up.

SECTION 7

Tips on being a leader

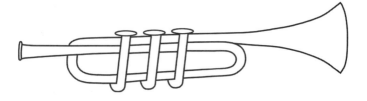

How to get band members to remember the day/time/places of gigs

I can't tell you how many times even the most responsible of band members has mixed up the day, time, or place of a gig. That is why it is so important that they get reminded of these items the day before the gig. Here are some other ways to spark their memory. Even if you try these approaches, you should still call each band member the day before the gig.

- At band rehearsal, hand each band member a gig sheet that lists the day, time, place, dress code (free drinks/food), and the pay. This way, they can never say "You never gave it to me," "I never got the email," "You didn't tell me the correct information over the phone," etc. Handing out the info in person and going over each item will ensure they have the correct information. I know they can always lose this piece of paper or think they can remember without checking, so even if you do hand out this info, I would still call them the day before the gig.

- You can call each band member and say, "Do you have your gig notebook handy so I can give you the day/time/place/pay etc. of the gig?" Have them write it all down and read it back to you. This way you both know it's written down right.

- You can email the band members, and make sure they reply to the email, so you know that they got it and it wasn't accidentally deleted by them or someone who lives with them. You don't want to hear at the gig, "Oh, I never got your email about not wearing jeans to this gig." You must get a reply from each band member. A band member can also say, "I never sent you a reply to that." In which case you show him the email with his reply (bring it with you); or if you don't bring it with you, tell him you will send that email to him later so he can see that, yes, he did reply to it.

If you can, rehearse at your house, which gives you more power

I've heard from so many band leaders that they feel more empowered rehearsing in their own houses. If they rehearse at a band member's house, that band member is likely to call the shots and run the band for the day. This doesn't always happen, but with domineering band members, it could very well happen. It's best to rehearse in your own house so you have control.

In extreme cases, dock their pay if they don't follow the rules

I haven't gotten to this point yet to dock someone's pay, but I have heard it is very effective if a band member does not follow rules. For example, let's say you want to control showing up late to a gig. You can say, "Anyone who shows up later than 15 minutes will be docked ten dollars from their pay." Interesting how toying with someone's money makes them shape up quickly. I've heard this tactic shapes up musicians fast.

If another band member books a gig, or all the gigs, remember this

As the leader, you must be aware that sometimes when another band member books the gigs, he may start trying to control the entire band.

We had two band members of ours book a gig. When we arrived, these two were doing a mini-gig as a duo with music that had nothing to do with the style of music we were to play that night. Even though they were doing their act before the gig started, the personnel at the bar assumed this was the type of music they would be getting all night. What I am saying to you is this: If someone else books the gig, be on watch at the gig that they don't take over in some way and usurp your power.

The good things about being a leader

Being a leader in a band will help you be a leader in any area of your life. You will learn how to speak up while being firm yet tactful, how to keep your calm in a crisis, how to wheel and deal with money if you are booking the gigs. You learn to be a great communicator. You will also learn to be a good listener, because your band members' opinions are important and may need to be implemented.

You will have the opportunity to learn to find the right balance between being too lax and being too much of a perfectionist. You will have the opportunity to become a good mediator between fighting musicians and do what is fair and just. You also will learn not to be co-dependent and let everyone walk all over you. This trait had better disappear once you become a band leader or you won't survive. You will gain respect by doing what you say you are going to do.

It's like having your own business; you are the president. You are responsible for the employees doing the job well. If your band shows up at a gig and some of them are late, not dressed correctly, or have attitude problems, this reflects on you. You have told the manager of the gig that they would be receiving a certain product, shall we say, and you have to make sure you deliver. The burden will lie with you. If the product you deliver is outstanding, you will have proven that what you said is what they got.

In our band, here is what we have the ultimate decision on

In our band we listen to everyone's input and are very open-minded and considerate, but we have the ultimate decision on:

- who we hire
- who we fire
- how we arrange the set list
- who will sing what songs (lead and harmony)
- what songs we will include in the set list
- what we put in a promo pak to send out (unless others are paying for it)

Who pays for the promo pak?

If no one in the band is contributing any money toward the promo pak and the leader has to pay for stamps, envelopes, photos, ink to print all the info, and phone calls to get gigs, the leader decides what is going to be in the promo pak. If you decide to have the band members contribute money toward the promo pak, the band members may want their input as to what picture goes in etc. They also may want to see receipts to make sure their money is being used for the promo pak. You'd be surprised that some leaders pocket some of the promo pak money for themselves. Yes, it does happen.

If you want to fire someone, tell him. Don't just say the gigs are canceled

We knew a band leader who told a band member the rest of the gigs they had were canceled. The gigs were not really canceled but the leader didn't know how to fire someone, so that is what he told him. It turns out the band member went to one of these "canceled" gigs and sure enough, there was the band up on stage. Don't be a bad, weak, cowardly leader like this.

When pay is concerned, stay true to your word

Don't be intimidated by the socio-economic position of another member or members of the band when it comes to getting paid. If you are a sideman, new member, or co-leader of a group, make sure that when you discuss how much you will be paid for an upcoming gig, you receive said amount after the gig. Usually, whoever books a gig assumes responsibility for disbursement of funds. In this case, we will now call him or her "the leader."

Let's assume all goes well and the club owner or party giver honors their oral or written contract and pays the leader the agreed-upon amount. So far, so good. However, let's say the leader decides at the last minute to hire a friend to shoot promo pictures at the gig for $100.00.

After the gig, everyone in the band is docked $10.00 to offset the photographer's fee and the leader expects you not to bat an eye. This is a problem. The leader who offers this largesse to his photographer friend without discussing taking $100.00 off the top has done something unethical. He may feel that it really doesn't make a lot of difference because, after all, it's only ten dollars. And it was done to help the band get more work, to boot. To him it may be chump change but he shouldn't assume others in the band would see it the same way. A band member might really need that ten bucks to buy gas to get home from the gig.

Keep your word as a leader when it comes to expected remuneration. As leader, it's best to cover a loss out of your own pocket in order to keep the rest of the band happy. Be sure to discuss any known pay adjustments/problems before anyone drives to the gig. This way, all the players know what to expect upfront when committing their time and energy to play a job.

If you don't show leadership skills, the band member who does will take over

If you don't show leadership skills, the musicians will gravitate toward the band member that does show these skills and follow him. Nothing worse than starting your own band and find out you are no longer the leader of it. Your band members could even try to fire you!

It's fun to be a leader, and it will empower you!

If you are meant to be the leader of a band, you will find it rewarding, empowering, and so much fun—despite any problems you may encounter. You will be your own boss and in control. Study the lives of great leaders in any field and learn from them. Don't be the type of boss everyone hates. Be the kind of leader everyone respects, admires, and loves to be around.

SECTION 8

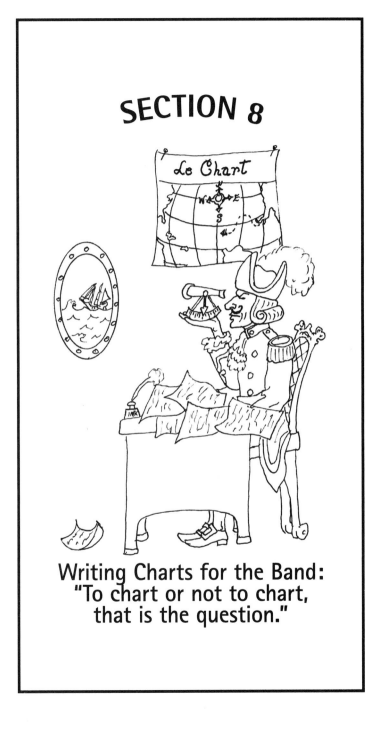

Writing Charts for the Band:
"To chart or not to chart,
that is the question."

I have decided to chart out all the songs that the band plays. This is because we have had a lot of different players come through the band and have had last minute subs cover various situations. Having a chart (lead sheet, master rhythm part, or lyric + chords chart) really helps get through a lot of turnover, if you will, when you are playing a lot of gigs. Even if you are fortunate enough to have the same personnel for years and have your sets down cold, having charts of your band's repertoire still gives you a sense of security over the future of the group. Also, when presenting new material to the band, you as a leader have expedited this process considerably because the chords and complete form of the song are documented on paper. You won't have to take rehearsal time to learn all the elements of the song from a recording. Hand out the chart and play the recording as the musicians follow along. One pass on listening is all you will need if you have prepared the chart correctly, as opposed to many repetitions during rehearsal with no chart.

I don't photocopy tunes from sheet music. The chart you prepare should be one or two pages maximum with an easy-to-read "roadmap" (form) of the song. Sheet music is difficult to read because it's usually written with three staves—a piano grand staff and a melody line—and can be four to six pages long. When you make a chart, be conscious of writing four bars to each line and beginning sections at the beginning of a line(don't bury them in the middle of a staff). Sheet music does not do this. A good chart is easy to read and follows the natural phrasing of the song's structure, usually four bar phrases.

This brings up a controversial subject: If the leader of the band does all the charts, should the individual band members bother to get their own charts together? It depends on the musician. Some players are well-versed in the style of the songs you play and only need music or a lyric and chord sheet to guide them through the song form and refresh them on a couple of chords. This is the best case scenario. Less acceptable is the feeling a band member may get that all the work has been done for him or her and that listening to the original tune is unnecessary. For example, this is especially true on Elvis tunes because of their simplicity. I look at 50's tunes as if they were classical music. To interpret them really requires some intimacy with the original recording to understand the style and use of simple major and minor chords.

Some musicians feel they should "dress up" or "improve" a simple Buddy Holly or Elvis tune to make it sound hipper or more up-to-date. As I said, I look at these songs as classical music that should be interpreted in an appropriate stylistic manner. If you deliberately change or enhance the original style to improve on the song as James Taylor and Linda Ronstadt did with Buddy Holly, and Brazil '66 did with the Beatles, that's a different story. It's a conscious, thought-out original arrangement meant to compliment the original composition. Some musicians may not like a certain song, and sarcastically dress it up with chord extensions, distortion, echo effects and the like. When you, as a leader, have invested a certain amount of time doing your homework, you can only expect other band members to do the same and learn their appropriate parts.

In the case of the musician who is unfamiliar with tunes outside of his comfortable style of playing, I would say, "You can use my charts as a reference until you can get your own charts together." This will give him a reason to dig into the original recordings and really listen to what's being played on his instrument. Don't be afraid to talk to a musician after a gig and say, "You know, you need to listen to the keyboard part on such-and-such a song. What you're playing doesn't capture the style of the keyboard part on the original session." Do this as often as you feel necessary, until you feel satisfied the 40+ songs in your set lists are played well enough.

A word of caution: Don't push too hard on this, or the main thing on that player's mind will be to leave your group! Every musician has a definite conception of what direction in music he or she feels they need to pursue. It's very personal and deep, and depending on the musician, too much constructive criticism can seem like a straightjacket. On the other hand, if as a group you are all on the same page about authenticity of style, it's just a fun exercise in getting a bunch of 3- to 4-minute songs down so people will like them!

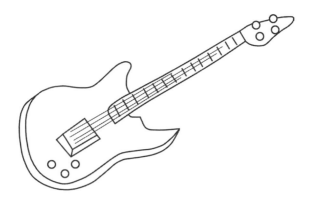

Well, there you have it.
What we have learned from our first hand experiences.
Hope this book has helped you.
We wish we had a book like this when we started out!

Questions or comments may be sent to our email address
which is listed on the Ordering Information page
which is at the back of this book.

PEACE

ANGELA'S POEMS

THE SUNSET OF LOVE

Red skies, like no place on earth
Transforming my demons, mystic rebirth
Shedding the old, creating the new
Flaming a passion for living renewed
Trials are full of intense, scorching heat
Lessons are hard but victory is sweet
Piercing hot rays of the sun in my cells
Vitality flowing, keeping me well
The orange-ruby sky talks to me now
Filling my heart full of love somehow
Like a torch I must carry for others to see
The sunset of love has now become me!

MOONBEAMS OF LOVE

Like an opal, shimmering ball
Above the sparkling stars
The moon secretes her charm
Over lovers near and far
Enchanting, mellow rays
Reach out for those who ask
To see their true love clearly
Behind romantic masks
And for those who have no love
Or perhaps a broken heart
A special moonbeam shines on you
To bring a new sweetheart!

MUSICAL BIOS
OF JOHN AND ANGELA TAYLOR

John and Angela have written and performed music that has been used by cable television shows, such as "Fishing the Emerald Coast" episodes and their theme song, Onyx Jewelry worldwide videos, and software and CD-ROM companies. Ten of John and Angela's songs have been picked up by three different music publishers. John Taylor (aka Kohlbacher) was trumpet player/arranger for The Charlie Daniel's Band and toured with them throughout the United States and Canada while the band's top ten hits were on the charts. John played trumpet for "Walt Disney's New Mickey Mouse Show," backed up The Temptations and other famous acts on trumpet, performed on many cruise ships and in orchestras. The Taylors currently perform in their own original jazz band, The John Taylor Project, and their oldies band, The Babyboomers. John has his master's degree in Music and attended Northwestern University, Eastman School of Music and California State University, Northridge. John holds a California Teaching Credential.

TO ORDER A COPY OF THIS BOOK:

Check out your local bookstore, music store or
record store. Or go to: Amazon.com

To Buy the Authors' CD of Original Music:
"A Goldmine of Melodies & Holiday Tunes"

Go to: www.klarity.com
Or call: (888) 387-8273
Or mail a check or money order to:
Klarity,
PO Box 160
North Vassalboro, ME 04962

To contact John and Angie with questions or comments:
musicalhearts@yahoo.com

To contact the artists for this book:
artgraphics@juno.com
blakston@saber.net

For Internet drum lessons: Visbeats.com